MW00943133

I Am V.A.L.

I Am V.A.L.

A 14 DAY DEVOTIONAL ABOUT LIVING
VALUED, ACCEPTED, AND LOVED!

*We have this hope as an anchor for the soul,
firm and secure. Hebrews 6:19a*

LaNette Jewel

XULON PRESS

Xulon Press
2301 Lucien Way #415
Maitland, FL 32751
407.339.4217
www.xulonpress.com

© 2021 by LaNette Jewel

Contribution by Stephanie Feagins

All rights reserved solely by the author. The author guarantees all contents are original and do not infringe upon the legal rights of any other person or work. No part of this book may be reproduced in any form without the permission of the author.

Due to the changing nature of the Internet, if there are any web addresses, links, or URLs included in this manuscript, these may have been altered and may no longer be accessible. The views and opinions shared in this book belong solely to the author and do not necessarily reflect those of the publisher. The publisher therefore disclaims responsibility for the views or opinions expressed within the work.

Unless otherwise indicated, Scripture quotations taken from the Holy Bible, New International Version (NIV). Copyright © 1973, 1978, 1984, 2011 by Biblica, Inc.™. Used by permission. All rights reserved.

Scripture quotations taken from the New King James Version (NKJV). Copyright © 1982 by Thomas Nelson, Inc. Used by permission. All rights reserved.

Scripture quotations taken from the Holy Bible, New Living Translation (NLT). Copyright ©1996, 2004, 2007 by Tyndale House Foundation. Used by permission of Tyndale House Publishers, Inc.

Scripture quotations taken from the New American Standard Bible (NASB). Copyright © 1960, 1962, 1963, 1968, 1971, 1972, 1973, 1975, 1977, 1995 by The Lockman Foundation. Used by permission. All rights reserved.

Scripture quotations taken from the Gods Word Translation copyright ©1995 by Baker Publishing Group.

Paperback ISBN-13: 978-1-66282-318-3

Ebook ISBN-13: 978-1-66282-319-0

TABLE OF CONTENTS

Dear Sister in Christ,

Have you ever felt devalued, unaccepted, or even unloved? Me, too. Words of degradation or condemnation roll off the tongues of others and cut us to the core. If this happens occasionally, an apology from the offender can help restore a relationship. Forgiving someone and extending them grace can help us heal from any pain caused by the original offense. Afterall, we all endure bad days from time to time and say and do things that hurt others, right? On the flip side, however, if the abuse is chronic and we are mistreated and belittled over a long period of time, it can wear us down and defeat us. If that's you, there's a good chance you began to believe the lie that says "_____, (Fill in your name) you will never measure up or be worth anything to anyone in this world." Therefore, you have learned to put a smile on your face, hoping it blinds people to the fact that there are gaping wounds in your soul that you fear will never heal. If that's you, then "Welcome to Val's House!" Come on in, kick off your shoes, take off your mask, make yourself at home and let's get real.

Val's House is a faith-based ministry named in honor of a young lady that lost her life tragically at age 20. Her name was Valarie but we called her Val. We use her name as an acronym so every woman who attends a meeting, retreat, or conference, will prayerfully come to know she is Valued, Accepted, and Loved, no matter what she has been through or is going through!

Thank you for taking this 14-day adventure with us. We pray the message of each day will connect your heart to the heart of our Father. May the Word of God, and the personal testimonies shared, encourage you to hunger for a personal encounter with the Holy Spirit. I will share part of my journey with you, and how losing Valarie, even though it was the darkest period my life, taught me the depth of God's love and faithfulness; and why I chose to serve him with my whole heart, broken as it was. Jesus really does work all things to the good for those who love him and are called according to his purpose. (Romans 8:28) As you read each day and reflect on the questions asked, reflect on your own life and ask Holy Spirit to speak to your heart. Answer them honestly and let the King of Glory lead you to hope and healing for your life no matter what you've been through. As we dive into the pages ahead together, let's dare to believe God has a purpose for your life that includes using your story; the good, bad, and ugly parts of it, for your good and His glory! May we all discover and proclaim "I am V.A.L."

Anchored in Hope,
LaNette Jewel
Founder, CEO
Val's House International Ministries

DAY
One

I am NOT Broken

He heals the brokenhearted and binds up their wounds. Psalms 147:3 (NIV)

The Lord is close to the brokenhearted and saves those who are crushed in spirit. Psalms 34:18 (NIV)

Have you ever felt like life has beaten you down? Perhaps a situation left you feeling defeated, crushed, broken. Maybe it happened in the past, maybe it is something you are dealing with right now. Regardless, your heart is broken. I'm sure most, if not all, of us could say "Been there, done that," or "Am there, doing that." Life deals us heartbreak at times. Whether at the hands of someone else, or by our own poor choices, we find ourselves experiencing the devastation

1

of brokenness. From my own experience, and the messages in scripture, however, I don't believe it has to *remain* devastating. Yes, life hurts sometimes, I am not dissing the pain we experience. It's real and it hurts. But there's good news! Jesus heals the broken hearted. Jesus can and will heal your broken heart. In fact, He calls the broken-hearted blessed.

> Matthew 5:4 says *"Blessed are those who mourn, for they shall be comforted." (NIV)*

We tend to think of mourning as grieving the death of a loved one, anguishing over a negative health diagnosis, or dealing with something that brings extreme sadness. In the midst of those experiences, we absolutely mourn. Mourning is these things, but so much more, as well. To fully grasp what Jesus meant by *"Blessed are those who mourn,"* let's look at the verse above it.

> Matthew 5:3 says *"Blessed are the poor in spirit, for theirs is the kingdom of heaven." (NIV)*

The poor in spirit are those that realize they are profoundly broken people in need of the saving grace of God. They recognize their need for Jesus as Savior and understand that He is our only hope. Once we understand how far we fall short, we experience a deep sense of mourning. If you're asking the question, "Why does Jesus say BLESSED are those that mourn."

Is it possible to be blessed by mourning our shortcomings? YES! Because in mourning, we experience the forgiving grace of God. In this comes the sweet promise that God Himself will bring us comfort when we mourn. God forgives us when we repent of our mistakes. God comforts us. He assures us that we are His, our forgiveness is secure, and that nothing can separate us from His love.

Isn't it astounding that we can experience the absolute comfort of our gracious God who holds our broken hearts? Whether our hearts are broken from death, disease, abuse, or from the realization of our own faults and blunders, the truth is, He breathes hope and healing into our lives. Will you choose to let Him heal your broken heart and bring you comfort today? Are you ready to yield your pain to Him? He already bore your pain on the cross. It's too heavy for us to carry, so let's not try any longer!

What brokenness do you need to surrender to Him today?

_____

_____

_____

As you relinquish your broken heart to Him, He will comfort you and fill you with hope and joy. The choice is yours. Will you choose to walk healed and whole? We are rooting for you! *You can do all things through Christ who gives you strength. Philippians 4:13 (NIV)*

What would you like to say to Jesus today?

_____

_____

_____

What Jesus is saying to you today: *I have loved you with an everlasting love, therefore I have drawn you with loving devotion.*

DAY
Two

I am NOT Rejected

What then shall we say in response to these things? If God is for us, who can be against us? Romans 8:31 (NIV)

*R*ejection. We've all experienced it in one form or another. Your spouse leaves you. You're overlooked for a promotion. Your opinions or ideas are not valued. You aren't invited to a party. You're bullied. No matter where it comes from, rejection can cause profound damage to the way we see ourselves, causing doubt and unbelief to creep in. When seeds of rejection are planted, they produce a harvest of failure. It can even affect our relationship with God. We may believe that if others don't like us, God won't either, or if people reject us, we may think God will shun us, too!

After all, He sees all of our faults, right? If He knows all of our weaknesses and shortcomings, shouldn't we expect that He will reject us, too?

That's what the enemy of our soul would like us to think but that goes against what scripture says about this. Here's the truth:

> *"To the praise of the glory of His grace, by which He has made us accepted in the Beloved." Ephesians 1:6 (NKJV)*

By grace, He has made us accepted!

You are not God's beloved because of what you do; it is Christ who did everything. He is God's Beloved. But God put you in Christ. That is why you are "accepted in the Beloved." Isn't that beautiful?

So, if the devil says to you, "How can you call yourself 'God's beloved' after what you just did?" you can have the assurance that being accepted is not based on what you have done, but what Christ has done. You are still God's beloved because you are in Christ!

Here's further proof that God accepts you.

> *"See, I have engraved you on the palms of my hands; your walls are ever before me." Isaiah 49:16 (NIV)*

That's a great picture of His love and devotion to you. Your name is etched on the palm of His hands and He is continually watching over you.

To put things into perspective, if anyone was ever rejected, it was Jesus Christ Himself. You can find many scriptures that discuss it but here are a couple to help us remember that Jesus experienced the same things that you and I do.

> *"He is despised and rejected by men, a Man of sorrows and acquainted with grief." Isaiah 53:3a (NKJV)*

> *"Surely He has borne our griefs and carried our sorrows." Isaiah 53:4a (NKJV)*

> *"He came to His own people, and even they rejected Him." John 1:11 (NLT)*

Being rejected is brutal. Sometimes the only way out of it is to go through it. Can you imagine the rejection Christ must have felt as He was beaten, flogged, then crucified by the very people He loved enough to die for? However, He chose for love to trump rejection. Why else would He have looked down from the cross at the very people who ripped His beard out, or hammered the nails in His hands and feet and say, "Forgive them Father, for they know not what they do?"

Does this reality give you the strength and courage to overcome your own rejection? _____

Why or why not? _____

_____

You may never get an apology from those who treated you so horribly. Is it enough to know that you are not truly rejected at all but you <u>ARE</u> accepted in the Beloved? _____

_____

How does this Greek definition of "accepted" help you receive the gift of God's grace? It means "to make graceful, charming, lovely, agreeable, to surround with favor and to honor with blessings?" WOWZER! What are your thoughts about yourself now?

_____

Do you see yourself as acceptable to God and will you accept His grace and let Him surround you with favor and blessings?

_____

_____

_____

Jesus' thoughts toward you: "You are NOT rejected! You ARE accepted into the Beloved! Since I am the Beloved, it means you are in me and I am in you! Don't let anyone's words or actions define you except Mine! I love you dearly and deeply! Don't ever forget that "greater is He who is in you that he who is in this world."

DAY
Three

I am NOT Unworthy

*But God showed his great love for us by sending
Christ to die for us while we were still sinners.
Romans 5:8 (NLT)*

roken. Rejected. Mocked. Shunned. Judged.
Unworthiness. Maybe you've experienced these, too.
I have. I can imagine the Woman at the Well did, too. Follow
me to John 4 and let's check this woman out!

Most believers are familiar with this popular Bible story as
recorded in John 4:1-40. We may surmise that she deserved to
be prejudiced against and find it perfectly acceptable that she
be shunned by her community. After all, she had been married
five times and was now, in fact, living with a man outside of
marriage. No wonder she had to go to the well in the heat of

the day for water, the other women didn't allow her to hang with them when they went in the cool of the day. She deserved this treatment, right? Or did she? What do we see when we take a deeper look? We see what's more important, the heart of Jesus. He is a loving and accepting God, and we should follow his example.

His encounter with the woman at the well broke three Jewish customs. First, he spoke to her even though she was a woman. Second, not only was she a woman but she was a <u>Samaritan</u> woman. (The Jews typically despised Samaritans.) Third, drinking from her cup or jar would have made him ceremonially unclean in their culture. But Jesus didn't care about all of that. What did he care about? Her!

Jesus' behavior probably shocked the woman, but she was forever changed that day. I hope you'll read the story from John 4 because there's so much more to this beautiful story than we can reflect on today. In summary, she was set free of her past when she encountered the love of Jesus that day. She ran back to her village with her soul cleansed and her spirit soaring and couldn't wait to tell people about Jesus. Yes, the same people who laughed at her, used her, and treated her as an outcast were now her audience of hope. "He told me everything I ever did." Many believed and went to the well to see him. After meeting Jesus, they said to the woman, "Now we believe, not just because of what you told us, but because we have heard him ourselves. Now we know that he is indeed the Savior of the world." (John 4:39-42 NKJV)

It is our human tendency, unfortunately, to judge people because of stereotypes or because they don't 'measure up' to our standards. Jesus treats us as individuals, with a love and compassion that overshadows our shortcomings. He doesn't love some and not others because they have, or have not, lived up to his expectations. Truth is, we all goof up and fall short of the glory of God (Romans 3:23). Yet, as our Bible verse today points out, it is while we are *still* goof-ups, that He died for us.

Take a moment to reflect on a time (or times) you felt judged and ridiculed. Remember how painful that was? Whether you were guilty or not, hurtful words spoken, negative actions taken, or toxic deeds performed against you, cut to the core and can become etched on your heart and soul for a lifetime. They can cause you to doubt or even hate yourself for the rest of your life. They certainly can rob you of your destiny if they are not dealt with.

However, there is hope! We all need an encounter with Jesus just like our friend at the well did. A place to safely talk about our broken lives without being judged or defined by them. A place where the love and compassion found in the eyes and arms of Jesus make all things new, restore our joy, and hope becomes the anchor of our soul that gives us the strength to face each day with enthusiasm.

Spend some time with Jesus right now and have that discussion with him at your "well." Share about that encounter with him.

_____

_____

_____

Let him quench your thirst with his living water. Oh, how refreshing it is! How do you feel now?

_____

_____

_____

My friends, there is one more thing I believe Jesus wants us to confront right now. Yes, we've all been hurt and can identify with the woman at the well. If we're honest with ourselves, though, I wonder how many times we've been the towns people; who mocked, made fun of, or been mad at someone else and thought it was our right to slay them with horrible, hurtful words or treat them as unworthy outcasts because we judged them for not living up to our expectations? Is there one or more people in this world who may be carrying around bleeding hearts or experiencing gaping wounds in their souls because of your bad behavior against them? I had to confront that reality in my own life too. There's love, compassion, grace, and mercy for us in these instances, too. List the names of those you've wronged, ask God to forgive you for judging and hurting them, then write a prayer asking God to release healing and restore hope and joy to them. You may need to do this on a separate sheet of paper if needed.

_____

_____

_____

Also, forgive yourself for falling short. We are *all* imperfect, but that isn't a surprise to Jesus. Remember, it is while we were *still* sinners, He died for us. I'd say that makes each of us worthy, don't you? He loves you so much. Write any final thoughts you have about how much he loves you and loves others. How has this lesson challenged you to be thankful for God's amazing grace in your own life? Has it challenged you to extend grace to others when they fall short? Share your thoughts.

_____

_____

_____

You are NOT broken, you ARE healed!

You are NOT rejected, you ARE worthy!

You are NOT unworthy, you ARE MOST DEFINITELY WORTHY!!!

DAY
Four

I AM Valued

Indeed, the very hairs of your head are all numbered. Do not fear; you are more valuable than many sparrows. Luke 12:7 (NASB)

There are reminders all around us of the value of God's creation. Consider the changing of the seasons, new life in the springtime and the beauty of fall colors. We marvel over the newness of the dawn and we watch in awe as God paints beautiful sunsets to close out our day. Even considering all of this beauty, the thing God values the most is you and me. All things in creation have purpose, but we were created for a personal relationship with God Himself. Zechariah 2:8 (ESV) says "... he who touches you touches the apple of his eye." Nothing, NOTHING is more valuable to God than you! Yes, YOU!!!

There is a song by Pat Bennett called "Canvas and Clay." The words of this song and the words from God in Psalm 139:14 (NASB) resonate, "I will praise you because I have been remarkably and wonderfully made. Your works are wonderful, and I know this very well." Please listen to the song and as you do, may its resounding theme help you see the perfect picture of God's love and how valuable you are to Him.

Perhaps something has happened in your life that prevents you from believing that God made you *remarkably* well and that you *are* valued, valuable, and worthy of that value? We've all had someone speak unkind things to us or about us and even mistreat us horribly. However, from this moment forward, let's don't give negative words a place in our heart and soul! Why should we when we now know the truth from God's lips! We ARE valued!!! YOU are valued!

"When I doubt it, Lord, remind me, I'm wonderfully made. You're an artist and a potter, I'm the canvas and the clay."

What thoughts or emotions come over you as you read those words?

_____

_____

_____

Let this serve as an anthem when doubt comes upon you. God made you because He loves you and wants a relationship with you. He is <u>ALL IN</u> and His love does not waiver. At times we walk with Him and at other times He carries us. Matt 10:31(NASB) "So do not fear; you are more valuable than many sparrows." What an honor it is to be considered valuable by God.

Father, thank you for loving me and valuing every hair that is on my head.

Help me to see the value that You see in me, Amen.

DAY
Five

I AM Accepted

And the grace of our Lord was more than abundant, with the faith and love which are found in Christ Jesus. It is a trustworthy statement, deserving full acceptance, that Christ Jesus came into the world to save sinners, among whom I am foremost of all. I Tim 1:14-15 (NASB)

It's a great feeling to be accepted by someone or a group of people that you may wish to be part of. It makes us feel wanted, like we belong. It's important and very much needed! However, Job reminds us that acceptance isn't always about accepting the good, but also to embrace the "not so good," too.

Job 2:10 (NASB) "Shall we indeed accept good from God and not accept adversity?"

Wow, thanks for that Job. (Insert sarcasm.) Seriously though, it's a good reminder that even in our darkest hour, God accepts us just as we are. Everything can be used for God's glory, *everything!* Don't get discouraged when adversity comes; look to the Lover of your soul and be grateful that God has not left you, but is right there beside you, willing to walk with you through the difficulty. Let's face it, His love for us is so true, so deep, that He never hesitates to lift us up and carry us when we have become so weary that we fear we can't take another step on our own. He knows the good, bad, and ugly about us, yet he sweetly challenges us...

> *Be strong and courageous. Do not be afraid or terrified because of them, for the LORD your God goes with you, he never will leave you, nor forsake you.* Deuteronomy 31:6 (NIV)

You have probably read this poem a hundred times, but let's read it again and this time, let's purposefully reflect on the level of intimacy Jesus has for each of us.

Footprints in the Sand

One night I had a dream...I dreamed I was walking along the beach with the Lord, and across the sky flashed scenes from my life. For each scene I noticed two sets of footprints in the sand. One belonged to me, and the other to the Lord. When the last scene of my life flashed before us, I looked back at the footprints in the sand. I noticed that many times along the path of my life, there was only one set of footprints.

I also noticed that it happened at the very lowest
and saddest times in my life.
This really bothered me, and I questioned the Lord about it.
"Lord, you said that once I decided to follow you,
You would walk with me all the way;
But I have noticed that during the
most troublesome times in my life,
There is only one set of footprints.
I don't understand why in times when I
needed you the most, you should leave me.
The Lord replied, "My precious, precious
child. I love you, and I would never,
never leave you during your times of
trial and suffering. When you saw only one set of footprints,
It was then that I carried you.

Do you see that image in your mind, Him carrying you through seasons of adversity? Get personal with Jesus right now. Ask Him to jog your memory of a time when you know He swept you up in His arms and carried you through a devastating, demanding, or heart wrenching time in your life.

_____

_____

_____

Thank Him for accepting you in all seasons of your life and for being willing to either walk with you or carry you through them. Thank Him also for never leaving you or forsaking you, even when you felt you were all alone.

_____

_____

_____

DAY
Six

I AM LOVED

For God so loved the world, that He gave His only begotten Son, that whoever believes in Him shall not perish, but have eternal life. For God did not send the Son into the world to judge the world, but that the world might be saved through him.
John 3:16-17 (NASB)

ears ago, my daughters went to a church camp where the theme was "Love God, Love Others."

At that time, we had a small dog named Snickers. It would be an understatement to say Snickers was not particularly fond of everyone in the family, and that feeling was reciprocated by the family. However, he loved me dearly. Everyone knew how much I loved Snickers so when the girls got back from camp, they adopted this saying. "We love Mom and Mom loves Snickers, therefore, we love Snickers." I was thrilled to learn that they extended the "Love God, Love Others" principles to this persnickety little pooch who did not return their affections!

I have pondered this many times over the years. How true it's been for all of us, I'm sure, to be "Snickers" at some point in our lives. You see, Snickers didn't lose sleep over the fact that no one cared for him except for me. I was enough to cause his little world to be full of peace and contentment. This challenges me so much. There have been situations in my life where I was not necessarily liked by everyone, or anyone for that matter. I wish I could say that, like Snickers, it didn't matter to me who did or did not like me, because the One True love I did have, Jesus, was enough. When He is our portion, we become enough; and that can be true even in our own hearts and minds. We then can compare ourselves to no one and we don't lose sleep over what others think of us because we know that we know that we know He loves us, and that is all that matters. We can be surrounded by negative people, storms can take place all around us, but when we realize that we are truly valued, accepted, and above all, LOVED, we can be fully at peace, fear-free!

> *So that Christ may dwell in your hearts through faith, and that you, being rooted and grounded in love, may be able to comprehend with all the*

*saints what is the width and length and height
and depth, and to know the love of Christ which
surpasses knowledge, that you may be filled up
to all the fullness of God. Eph. 3:17-19 (NASB)*

The word love is mentioned in the Bible between 500-800 times. 1 Cor.13:7 (GW) "Love never stops being patient, never stops believing, never stops hoping, never gives up." The same love that God gives to you, he wants you to offer to everybody else that you encounter. This is not an option or a suggestion, it is a command from Jesus, himself: John 13:34 (NLT) "Now I am giving you a new commandment: Love each other. Just as I have loved you, you should love each other."

Mark 12:31 (NASB) personalizes this, "You shall love our neighbor as yourself." Some of us may have a harder time with this phrase. How can you love others if you do not love yourself or believe, "I Am Loved?"

With all that is happening in this world, know and remember this one thing: for God so loved YOU, that He gave up His Son for YOU. If YOU believe in Him, YOU will not perish, but have eternal life with Him.

Ponder this: Is there a "Snickers" in your life right now? Maybe they are hard to love, set in their ways, or just plain obnoxious. Maybe they don't like you. Just like my family adopted the saying, "We love Mom and Mom loves Snickers, therefore, we love Snickers". Remember, we've all been 'Snickers' before. We all needed the assurance that we are truly loved. Will you make an effort to show the "Snickers" in your life that "I love God, God loves you, therefore, I love you!" list some ways you can accomplish this:

_____

_____

_____

Lord, thank you for loving me unconditionally. I don't deserve it, but you freely give it. Help me to extend to others that same love, and may they find true peace and contentment in You!

DAY
Seven

TAKE THIS CUP

"Father, if you are willing take this cup from me..."
Luke 22:42a (NIV)

Have you ever had a "Gethsemane" experience? A moment, experience, or season in your life that was so agonizing that you cried out to God, "Please God, don't make me go through this?" I'm sure most of us have. I can't say my life has been an easy one, quite the opposite, actually. But there is one particular event that was my defining moment as a believer. I had a choice to make: be mad at God and turn my back on Him or choose to fully surrender to Him and trust Him to take this awful scenario and bring glory to Himself through it. I'll tell you more of my story in Day 10 but right now, let's focus on what Jesus went through. Understanding His own agony helps us put things into perspective when we suffer greatly in our own lives. Nothing we will ever go through, compares to what He went through for us.

Jesus knew when and how He was going to die.

The night before He was to be crucified, He shared the Lord's Supper with the disciples, then led them to the Garden of Gethsemane. He took Peter, James, and John deeper into the Garden with him where the Bible says he began to be deeply distressed and troubled. Try to imagine the depth of His agony in that moment when He says to His three closest friends,

> *"My soul is overwhelmed with sorrow...stay here*
> *and keep watch." Mark 14:33-34 (NIV)*

Can you fathom what the disciples were going through as well? Here is their best friend, Jesus, whom they personally and intimately knew as Teacher, Rabbi, Messiah. They had seen Him heal the sick, raise the dead, cast out demons, walk on water, silence storms, and feed thousands of people with a little boy's sack lunch. Yet, here He is, overwhelmed, knowing what is about to happen. I'm sure this was a side of Jesus they hadn't witnessed before. Vulnerable. Sorrowful. Agonized. Human.

> *Going a little farther, he fell to the ground and*
> *prayed that if possible, the hour might pass*
> *from him. "Abba, Father, everything is possible*

for You. Take this cup away from me.....” Mark 14:35-36a (NIV)

What event or circumstance in your life have you wished that God would simply take it away so you or your loved ones wouldn't have to suffer through it?

_____

_____

_____

Does today's reflection on the depth of the emotions and overwhelming sorrow Jesus experienced bring you comfort as you look on your own situation? _____ How so?

_____

_____

Prayer: Abba Father, just as you were with your Son in his final hours, you have been with me in times of sorrow and sadness as well. I am so grateful that you never leave me or forsake me, even though I have given you reason to do so. But rather, your presence goes with me and you give me rest. Help me to seek you daily with my whole heart. I love you, Jesus! Amen

> *The Lord replied, “My presence will go with you, and I will give you rest.” Exodus 33:14 (NIV)*

> *“You will seek me and find me when you seek me with all your heart.” Jeremiah 29:13 (NIV)*

DAY
Eight

GOD SEES THE BIG PICTURE

Then Job replied to the Lord, "I know that you can do all things, and that no purpose of yours can be thwarted. You asked, 'Who is this that obscures my plans without knowledge?' Surely, I spoke of things I did not understand, things too wonderful for me to know." Job 42:1-3 (NIV)

When life feels out of control, it's comforting to focus on the fact that we are never out of God's sight. He never loses control. Job was reminded of God's sovereignty and he humbly submitted to it, responding to God with remorse for his earlier words.

Job had lost everything. *EVERYTHING!* His children, all possessions, his health, and even his will to live. While he rightly defended himself against his friends' accusations of sin, he could not have known the purpose of God letting him suffer so deeply. God's "big picture" plan was to restore Job's prosperity and to double his possessions. Only God sees the big picture. It's our job to trust in His sovereignty.

Unlike Job, Jesus knew exactly what His future was. In a matter of hours, he would be spat upon, beaten and flogged, stripped naked and nailed to a cross. It's understandable why Jesus, being fully human, was crying out to the Father to take this cup from him. Yet, being fully God, He knew the big picture. He knew He must suffer these things or you and I would spend an eternity separated from the Father.

In Luke's account of this story, he says, "His sweat became like great drops of blood falling to the ground." We have all suffered tragedy at some level but think of what Jesus must have been going through as He awaited the final hours of His life. His agony reached such proportions that His capillaries began to burst, mixing blood with His sweat. He began to bleed before anyone had laid a hand on Him. It's no wonder He called out to His Father to remove this cup from Him if it was possible.

Jesus knew the big picture, but do we have the even the smallest idea of His great love for us?

Imagine if you will, Jesus praying in the Garden. Do you see Him? Eyes fixed on Heaven, crying out to His Father to remove the cup of suffering from Him? Do you see the blood and sweat that has fallen to the ground around Him because of intense prayers that caused blood vessels to pop? How does this image of Christ help you understand the depth of torture and suffering He knew awaited Him? Does it help you understand how deeply He loves you? How does it affect the way you will love and serve Him from this moment forward?

_____

_____

_____

DAY
Nine

NOT MY WILL, BUT YOURS

"...yet not my will, but yours be done." Luke 22:42b (NIV)

*J*esus didn't simply pray for this cup of wrath to pass from him if it was at all possible. He prayed so intently that sweat drops of blood fell from his body, Yet, the words He spoke next, "Not my will, but yours be done" is the most remarkable example of faith and trust in the Father. Jesus knew what awaited Him; betrayal, beatings, the flogging, carrying the cross on his mutilated back to Golgotha, and the most horrific, humiliating death possible: crucifixion. Yet, fully knowing this, He chose to surrender His will to His Father's will.

What exactly does it mean to surrender to God? Surrender is a battle term and implies giving up all rights to the conqueror.

When an opposing army surrenders, they lay down their arms, and the other side takes control over them. Surrendering to God is similar. God has a plan for our lives, and surrendering to Him means we lay down our own plans and eagerly seek His.

Sounds simple, right? In reality it is not. Surrendering our will is a constant battle for most of us, but it is for our good. Being fully surrendered to God means to be sold out or ALL IN; no more living on the fence, but desiring to live only to please Him. When we choose to live in obedience to Him, He takes away any chaos or mess we are dealing with internally and He replaces it with calmness, peace, and joy!

What area(s) of your life is filled with disorder or confusion?

_____

_____

_____

Ask the Holy Spirit if this is present in your life because you are holding out for your own will and not truly seeking His?

_____

Are you ready to pray as Jesus did? "...yet not my will, but Yours be done."

Pray this:

"Heavenly Father, in Jesus' name, please be the Lord of my life in every area today. I surrender my will to You and ask you to please make me humble. Grant me a heart that seeks after Yours in all things. I pray You get all the glory. I am all ears, Father, speak to me about the motivations of my heart, and guide my life so I seek Your will only, not my own selfish desires. Thank You, Father. In Jesus' name, amen."

DAY
Ten

FACING OUR PERSONAL GETHSEMANES

Then Jesus said to his disciples, "If any of you
wants to be my follower, you must give up your
own way, take up your cross, and follow me."
Matthew 16:24 (NLT)

s it truly possible to go all in with Jesus? No matter what? If we pick up our cross and follow Him, that means we experience His suffering as well as His victory. We live by His example, no matter the cost? Easier said than done, right? Yet, the cost any of us will ever pay to follow Him will never measure up to the cost He paid for us. He laid down His life for us, giving us His ALL. Was it easy for Him? Not at all. On Day 9, we discussed Jesus' prayer in the garden of

Gethsemane when he cried out for His Father to remove the cup of wrath that He was about to drink from. His suffering was real. His love for us, even more so.

Have you ever experienced a personal Gethsemane moment? Something so unthinkable happened, leaving you scared, emotionally paralyzed, and wondering if anything good could possibly come from something so devastating?

Today, I'd like to share with you my personal Gethsemane experience. This is the event in my life that drew a line in the sand for me. I had to make a choice, was I going to be angry at God and live a bitter existence? Or would I allow Him to mold me and prepare me for victory through it? I chose the latter. It wasn't easy, it still isn't, but oh, so worth going all-in with Jesus. Nothing happens without His knowledge, and nothing happens that He cannot use to bring healing and hope to us, and glory to Himself, if we are willing to trust Him with our heart and trust Him to guide our steps daily.

It was October 12, 1993 at approximately 10:15pm. My youngest sister, Valarie, had been missing all day. At the time she was 20 years old and dating a very nice young man, so naturally, at first, the family didn't think much about it when we couldn't reach her by phone. (This was before everyone had their own cell phones.) We assumed she was with her boyfriend and perhaps distracted by the whimsical moments that often accompany falling in love. We were happy for her. However, by late that night, we had all become very alarmed and sensed that something was horribly wrong.

I called the police and headed to her apartment. I arrived about 20 minutes later and was met by a slew of uniformed police officers and detectives. Three of them approached me and asked me if I was kin to Valarie Walker. I responded that I was her sister and tried to walk around them to go into her apartment. One of the officers put his arm up to stop me and said, "Ma'am, I can't let you go in there." When our eyes met, I knew intuitively what his words were going to be. He continued, "I'm sorry, your sister is dead." Nothing can prepare you for such devastating information. I remember my reaction like it happened five minutes ago. I turned around and collapsed, crying and screaming out, "No, no, no, not Valarie, Lord. No, no, no!" I repeated it over and over. The moment I stopped screaming though, I heard the voice of Jesus in my ear repeating what He said in His most dismal hour there in the Garden of Gethsemane, "Father, if possible, take this cup from me."

I know it seems strange to fathom but those words brought me immediate comfort because I realized two things. Number one, I was not alone, He met me there! On purpose. To hold me. To comfort me. His presence was strong, warm, and full of love. Number two, those words reminded me that even Jesus

Himself went through something He didn't want to do. You can only imagine how that settled me down and strengthened me to endure the things that were to come. After an hour and a half of detectives interrogating me and police officers asking questions about what they were finding in her apartment, I was finally told that she had been burglarized and strangled by an intruder. We eventually learned that he sold some of her jewelry and other belongings in exchange for a $75 hit of crack cocaine.

When law enforcement officers weren't asking me questions, the Lord continued to hold me and talk to me. His voice was tender, yet firm. He assured me that just as I experienced His presence learning of her murder that He also comforted her in her last moments. He told me not to worry about her, that she was with him and I would see her again someday. He said emphatically yet unapologetically, "Daughter, you see the little picture and it hurts. But I see the big picture and that's what I need you to be a part of." I knew He was calling me to go "all-in" with Him, totally surrendering my life so He could use this story for His glory and to impact the lives of many people along the way.

No words can express what it is like to experience such an atrocity as I did that night. At the same time, no words can express the personal and intimate presence and conversation that I experienced with Jesus in those same hours. It was horrific and beautiful all at the same time. It changed my life forever.

Years later the Lord led me to begin a faith-based ministry where women could gather in a nonjudgmental atmosphere and talk about the real aches and pains of life. No mask is needed, transparency is encouraged, and no judgment is allowed at our meetings. We talk openly and honestly and seek hope and healing for life's wounds in the unconditional love of Jesus Christ, the Power and Presence of Holy Spirit, and the Promises and Truth of God's Word! Together, we get to watch God mend hearts and mold legacies!

What does your heart need to mend from today?

_____

_____

_____

Will you allow Him access to your broken heart so His love can begin your healing journey?

You are not alone. Several bible verses record His promise, "I will never leave you, nor forsake you." Read several of them and then write your favorite one here.

_____

_____

_____

Write a prayer expressing your gratitude to Jesus for never leaving you or forsaking you.

_____

_____

_____

DAY
Eleven

CHOOSING ALL-IN

If you try to hang on to your life, you will lose it.
But if you give up your life for my sake, you will
save it. Matthew 16:25 (NLT)

Give up your life and you will save it. It's not the easiest thing to do, but going all in with Jesus, is living a life fully surrendered to Him! What do we get in return? For one thing, a life filled with unspeakable joy. Not going "all in" with Jesus is to merely acknowledge who He is without desiring to know Him personally. That will lead to a frustrated, discouraging spiritual life.

The story of the rich young ruler we read about in Matthew 19 is the perfect example of this. He desired to know Jesus but chose to not fully surrender to him when Jesus told him to go sell his possessions and give to the poor and he would have treasure in heaven. The young man went away sad because he had great wealth.

On the other hand, a great example of going "all in" for Jesus is Barnabas. Acts 4 says that he sold his field and gave the proceeds to the apostles. Barnabas went on to preach alongside Paul for many years, helped start churches throughout Asia Minor and Europe. Barnabas was able to make a huge impact on the world because he chose to go "all in" with Jesus. He became known as "a good man, full of the Holy Spirit and faith" (Acts 11:24).

Now that's a legacy to leave, right? Going "all in" not only affects our life but impacts generations to come. What legacy do you want to leave?

_____

_____

_____

Are you willing to go "all in?" _____ I believe most of us desire to. Perhaps what holds us back from making that commitment is knowing the areas of our lives that we haven't fully surrendered to Him. Maybe for some reason we aren't ready to surrender them. Some areas many struggle with are finances, addictions, sexual sin, or one that trips a lot of us up... forgiveness issues. What areas of your life have you not fully surrendered? Be honest with yourself. Jesus isn't going to judge you or be angry with you. He is going to be proud of you for admitting your weaknesses. He's always so excited about helping us be the overcomers we are called to be!

_____

_____

_____

If you need prayer or a confidante to share your struggles with, please reach out to a trusted friend or send us an email at vals_house@yahoo.com and we will be glad to pray with you.

We are able to go "all-in" when we understand that Jesus went "all-in" for us. Our God is an "all-in" God, and He has called and empowered us to be "all-in" people.

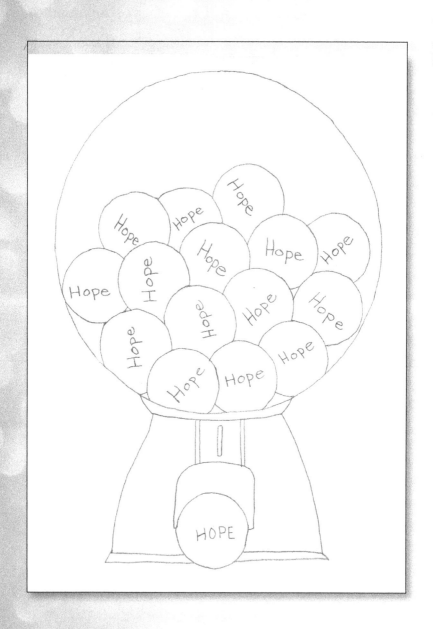

DAY
Twelve

OVERFLOWING WITH HOPE

"May the God of hope fill you with all joy and peace as you trust in him, so that you may over-flow with hope by the power of the Holy Spirit."
Romans 15:13 (NIV)

This is one of my favorite verses on hope. If I can be transparent with you, though, as I studied it in prepara-tion for this devotional, it convicted me about something. "Do you overflow with hope?" That's the question I asked myself. I didn't like the answer. Recently, it seemed my hope tank was running on empty. Unfortunately, I had been focusing on a sit-uation that was overwhelming me and I began to feel defeated. That's what happens when we become fixated on a situation when instead, we should have our eyes on the God of hope!

So then, what is the key to being filled with all joy and peace so we can overflow with hope? The verse answers that, too. Trust. In Him. So that you may overflow with hope by the power of the Holy Spirit.

As God so lovingly pointed out, joy, peace, and hope are intertwined with trusting in Him. If we are not filled with joy and peace or overflowing with hope, it's probably time to do a self-evaluation to see if there is an area of our life where we are not putting our trust in Him.

What about you? Are you overflowing with hope? Is hope bubbling up in you and spilling over onto those around you; inoculating them with joy and peace? What is the Holy Spirit saying to you about this?

_____

_____

_____

What is something you may not be trusting God with, that is preventing you from experiencing the overflow of hope?

_____

_____

_____

Talk to God about it. He is trustworthy. The more we walk with Him, the more this hope will overflow in our lives and others around us will notice.

If the God of hope has filled you with all joy and peace and you are overflowing with hope by the power of the Holy Spirit, do you know what that makes you? A Hope Dispenser!

Prayer: Father God, You alone are my source of hope! Thank you that as I trust you, I'll be filled with all joy and peace. I know I need to trust you more, please help me by showing me any area of my life where I am not fully trusting you. My desire is to overflow with hope by the power of the Holy Spirit.

Declaration: I am overflowing with hope because I trust God, because He fills me with all joy and peace.

Guess what, my friends, this makes *YOU* a *HOPE DISPENSER!!!*

DAY
Thirteen

I am a Hope Dispenser

This hope is a strong and trustworthy anchor for our souls. Hebrews 6:19a (NLT)

Hope. We all need it.

With the condition our world is in right now, there seems to be an influx of people living in fear, and in the midst of the turmoil, they feel hopeless. Sound familiar?

Whether it's the condition of our government, global concerns, divorce, illness, etc., one thing many of us have in common right now is that we are grasping for something that will give us hope. Hope that things will get better soon. Hope for finances to be restored. Hope that God will be with us during turbulent times. Hope for a better future.

Let's be encouraged as we reflect on why we as Christians can undeniably have hope in Christ. As it comes alive in you, so will a renewed vim, vigor, and strength to help you stay positive, even in the midst of the most difficult of situations and times. Not only that, He will use you as a "Hope Dispenser" to pour into others the hope we have found in Him. He truly is a strong and trustworthy anchor for our souls, as Hebrews 6 reassures us!

Having faith in Christ gives us hope in knowing that although the future may be uncertain, it *can* be entrusted to God. He *will* help us through.

Let's get personal for a moment. How is *your* hope? Does it help you bounce back or does it cause you to doubt and lose hope in a situation? God knows that we all struggle with finding and holding onto hope so there's not condemnation; only a challenge to reflect on our own personal walk with Christ. Let's face it, when perplexing times arise and tests of our faith come, even the strongest Christians can find it difficult to maintain hope. That's when we really need 'Hope Dispensers' to stand in the gap and speak life into us as they walk with us through seemingly hopeless times.

Sometimes we need Hope Dispensers and sometimes we need to *be* the Hope Dispensers, offering hope and encouragement to others. Which season are you in right now? ____

_____

If you need a Hope Dispenser, are you reaching out to a trusted confidante and asking them for encouragement? If not, are you willing to make that phone call right now? We all need somebody when life gets heavy. Who are you going to call? Do it now and record your thoughts and feelings after you do. Hopefully you feel strengthened and encouraged.

_____

_____

_____

Who in your life needs a Hope Dispenser right now? _____

_____

Will you fill that role for them right now? _____
Call and speak a word of life and encouragement to them and record their reactions.

_____

_____

_____

Way to go! You are now officially a Hope Dispenser! Keep up the good work!

People need you!

DAY
Fourteen

WRITE YOUR OWN
DEVOTIONAL TODAY

*A*sk Holy Spirit to give you a bible verse for what He wants to say to you. It may be one you've read in this devotional or it may be something completely different.

Let Him guide you.

_____

_____

_____

What has the Holy Spirit revealed to you during this 14-day adventure? Journal your thoughts, concerns, prayers, etc. Don't forget to thank God that you truly are Valued, Accepted, and Loved by Him, no matter what!!!!

_____
_____
_____
_____
_____
_____
_____
_____
_____
_____
_____
_____
_____
_____
_____
_____
_____
_____

If you haven't asked Jesus into your heart as Lord and Savior, there's no time like the present. If you are ready to do so, congratulations on the best decision of your life.

The following is taken from *Wild at Heart* by John Eldridge and will lead you in the prayer to receive Christ.

A Prayer to Receive Jesus Christ as Savior

The most important relationship for every one of us is our relationship with Jesus Christ. Choosing to believe that he is who he claimed to be—the Son of God and the only way to salvation— and receiving him by faith as your Lord and Savior is the most vital act anyone will ever do. We want life. He is Life. We need cleansing. He is the Living Water.

Here is a simple prayer if you have not yet given your life to Jesus and invited him into yours:

Jesus, I believe you are the Son of God, that you died on the cross to rescue me from sin and death and to restore me to the Father. I choose now to turn from my sins, my self-centeredness, and every part of my life that does not please you. I choose you. I give myself to you. I receive your forgiveness and ask you to take your rightful place in my life as my Savior and Lord. Come reign in my heart, fill me with your love and your life, and help me to become a person who is truly loving—a person like you. Restore me, Jesus. Live in me. Love through me. Thank you, God. In Jesus' name I pray. Amen.

Knowing that you are Valued, Accepted and Loved

*I*f you prayed to received Christ, welcome to God's family! Please email us and let us know of your decision to follow Christ.

Have questions, comments, or need someone to talk to or pray with? Email us and we'll get in touch with you.

Email us vals_house@yahoo.com.

Our website is www.valshouse.net

Click on 'About Us' and then 'Contact us' and you can leave messages there, as well.

Follow us on Facebook at Val's House Ministries, Twitter @ ValsHouse1, subscribe to our YouTube Channel at Val's House and enjoy our podcast, "Life with Me, Myself, and I AM!"

To donate to the ministry, go to www.valshouse.net, or give via Venmo @ValsHouseMinistires or Zelle at vals_house@yahoo.com

Final thoughts: Knowing that God loves us without boundaries and meets us in our darkest hour is proof enough for me that we all can confidently proclaim, "I am VAL!" Who is VAL? You are, my friend! You ARE Valued, Accepted, and Loved no matter what.

Thank you for sharing this 14-day journey with us. It has been our honor to serve you, grow with you, and become Hope Dispensers with you!

From our heart to yours,

LaNette Jewel
Founder and CEO
Val's House International Ministries

and

Stephanie Feagins
President and COO
Val's House International Ministries

ACKNOWLEDGEMENTS

From the Author's heart...

In all the years I have had the privilege of serving the Lord through Val's House Int/l Ministries, He has surrounded me with the greatest group of ladies that have served beside me. They give of their time and talents and roll up their sleeves and get in the trenches as needs arise. They are dedicated to Christ as His hands and feet day in and day out. They never look for kudos but I feel led to share these servants with you. Please join me in asking God to bless them big for their undying love and devotion to Him and Kingdom work. Thank you from the very bottom of my heart Diane Richmond, Barbara Rambo, Pat McClead, Sarah Hawkins, Samantha Sheffield, Shelle Diehm, Sherry Graves, Celeste Poppe, Sheila Madore, Kathie Tipping, Anita Sohn and Donnye Matthews for your servant hearts. No words express the depth of my gratitude!

Thank you, Barbara Rambo and Karen Hargrave, our amazing, talented artists.

God truly flows through you ladies, in your art and in your hearts.

Jenna Warford, you encourage and inspire me in so many ways. Thank you for your love, friendship, wisdom, sense of humor, and sharing your editing skills with us. You're the best!

To my children, Lindsay Hendrix and Timothy Hendrix, you bless me so much! You have both always been so supportive and my biggest cheerleaders. So often your words of encouragement and unparallel love have been the very thing that prevented be from giving up as we have endured difficult times. I love and adore you so much! You make this Mama proud!

Jesus, because of You we live knowing we are Valued, Accepted, and Loved by You! We'll never be the same. Please continue to bless and anoint us to love and lead Your children to the full knowledge of who You are; the hope we have as an anchor for the soul; firm and secure!

There is one more Val's Gal I would like to thank with a special acknowledgement.

This lady came to our first conference and we became fast friends, sassy sisters, partners in crime, and quite a dynamic duo when it comes to putting together conferences, retreats, podcasts (check out *Life with Me, Myself, and I AM* on YouTube) and much more.

Stephanie Feagins, thank you, thank you, thank you, for being able to read my mind, be my right arm, and keeping me focused and moving forward in our Kingdom call as Val's House. Your leadership and friendship mean so much to me. I truly have no words to describe the depth of my gratitude. I love you deeply!

CPSIA information can be obtained
at www.ICGtesting.com
Printed in the USA
LVHW051513270821
696161LV00004B/467

9 781662 823183